John Graver Johnson

A Criticism of Mr. Reed's Aspersions on the Character of Dr. Benjamin Rush

Vol. 1

John Graver Johnson

A Criticism of Mr. Reed's Aspersions on the Character of Dr. Benjamin Rush
Vol. 1

ISBN/EAN: 9783337293000

Printed in Europe, USA, Canada, Australia, Japan

Cover: Foto ©Thomas Meinert / pixelio.de

More available books at **www.hansebooks.com**

A CRITICISM

OF

MR. WM. B. REED'S ASPERSIONS

ON THE

CHARACTER OF DR. BENJAMIN RUSH,

WITH AN INCIDENTAL CONSIDERATION OF

GENERAL JOSEPH REED'S CHARACTER.

BY A

MEMBER OF THE PHILADELPHIA BAR.

"And he that stands upon a slippery place,
Makes nice of no vile hold to stay him up."—KING JOHN.

PHILADELPHIA:
COLLINS, PRINTER, 705 JAYNE STREET.
1867.

Henry B. Dawson

INTRODUCTION.

UNDERSTANDING that the descendants of Dr. Benjamin Rush will not reply to Mr. Wm. B. Reed's recent assault upon their ancestor, the writer, personally acquainted with many of them, and, as an American, indignant at Mr. Reed's attempt to depreciate the national inheritance in the fair fame of the Founders of our Independence, by exhibiting to the public as a true picture of one of these patriots, a portrait which, with no light other than that of a treacherous imagination, he has outlined by little stabs with a stiletto steeped in the gall of his passions, has felt impelled to do so himself and to unmask the real motives of the attack.

In doing this, however, he has ventured upon no systematic review of Mr. Reed's work, and has respected the feelings of those universally esteemed descendants of General Reed, who have never joined

4

in Mr. Wm. B. Reed's efforts to force their ancestor into an undue prominence, nor in his assaults upon those whom the sanctity of the grave should have shielded. He has therefore declined a discussion of the charge of treason so frequently made, 'and, in support of those he has considered, has neither searched for new materials, nor availed himself of old ones not already known to the public through the Cadwalader Pamphlet, and the "Life and Correspondence of Joseph Reed, by his Grandson."

J. G. J.

PHILADELPHIA,
13th May, 1867.

NOTE.

Mr. Benjamin Rush's Reply, which has been received since the completion of this Criticism, has removed one of the reasons which induced its preparation.

A CRITICISM

OF

MR. WM. B. REED'S ASPERSIONS.

THERE are, in this community, many who, whilst they might favorably consider an application for the defendant's pardon, in Commonwealth *vs.* Reed, have ever felt it their duty to frustrate, not only his accomplished "advocate's" unprofessional attempts to set aside a verdict, which has stood, for upwards of eighty-four years, unappealed from and unshaken, but still more his efforts to substitute for the notoriety which justly attached to his client the greatness which was not his due, by making astronomical observations in the Revolutionary sky through a telescope reversed whenever the Satellite Reed was not in the field of vision. They have done this by republishing, twice or thrice since 1847, the un-answered and unanswerable charges, specifications, and proofs, of the Cadwalader indictment.

There are others, however, of whom the writer, until recently, was one, who, in admiration of the untiring industry with which Mr. Reed has so long labored at his Herculean task of cleaning the Augean stable of his grandfather's reputation, and still more out of regard for the sanctity of the grave and the susceptibilities of the living, have felt no disposition to interfere with his endeavors to deceive the public as to the exceeding smallness of his patrimony in that particular in which, according to Horne Tooke, the children of Sir John Scott were so unfortunate. Such interference, however, has now become an imperative duty, since, not content quietly to submit to his failure to remove the remains of his ancestor from the Valley of Humiliation in which, though unhonored, they were mouldering undisturbed, to that Laurel Hill in which lie entombed only the "*accredited*" patriots of the Revolution, Mr. Reed has striven, in his revenge, to disfigure and overturn the monuments which the gratitude of posterity had erected over the honored dead.

During General Reed's lifetime he was publicly charged by a responsible accuser, upon adduced testimony, with,

First. Such cowardly disaffection during the month of December, 1776, whilst holding a responsible position in the American Army, as inclined him to consider favorably the propriety of applying for the protection offered by the British Commissioners to those who accepted it prior to January, 1777.

Second. An actual application for this protection.

This second count, for the reason given in the Introduction, will not be discussed. If, goaded into desperation by Mr. Bancroft's mere allusion to what, in the shape of formal charges and proofs in a pamphlet published upwards of eighty-four years ago, neither his ancestor, himself, nor any of his immediate descendants ever refuted, Mr. Reed has succeeded in demonstrating that his grandfather was unjustly accused of being a traitor, none more than the writer will rejoice. Though he may not desire to have General Reed canonized, even in the order of "Latter-Day Saints," he cannot, if he was innocent, sufficiently deplore the singular hardness of the fate by which, without concert or mutual knowledge, he became the victim of entries in private "Journals," of the adverse "rumors" of the enemy's camp, of the accusations of his countrymen, and of the harsh criticisms of travellers. How thoroughly Mr. Reed has succeeded in demolishing the "Donop Diary," and in convicting Mr. Bancroft of perversions and false assertions, with materials admitted to have been furnished by the "malicious defamer" himself; and how far, even upon his own version,* the words "Colonel Reed having received a protection" are to be taken as the statement, in

---

* Page 91 of Mr. Reed's Reply.

parenthesis, of a fact, or as a part of the rumors, must be for others to discuss and decide.

This charge, however, does not necessarily imply the existence of a treacherous *heart*. General Reed's sympathies must have ever been, not with the British, but with the people amongst whom his life had been passed; and if he was led astray, it must have been by his fears. If this "Reed," which the sun of King George's royal favor could not warp, was broken at last, it was not until after it had been "shaken by the winds" of adversity which swept with such terrible force over the sands and through the pines of New Jersey. Whilst he lay at Burlington, with his family safely disposed of, on that memorable December morning when the days of grace were so nearly numbered, he must have still hoped for news of such a victory for America as would render safe, in the future, adhesion to her cause. His "Pomroy" letter, though manifesting no desire to lead or even to join, the forlorn hope he counselled, shows an anxiety not only that it should be formed, but also that it should attack with success, before "the sixty days expire which the commissioners have allowed."

"There is in this country," says Mr. Reed, "a class of men, happily not numerous, who take pleasure in disparaging the *accredited* patriots of the first Revolution. They do so either from *hereditary or personal animosity*, or on a principle of paradox and contradic-

tion." Before attempting to demonstrate the truth
of Dr. Rush's statements concerning General Reed,
and the groundlessness of Mr. W. B. Reed's attacks,
which will involve an incidental consideration of the
first of the above counts, it will be shown that the
attack was unnecessary and unprovoked, and could
only have originated in the instincts of one of the
class which Mr. Reed, fearlessly disregarding the
odium attaching to the accomplice-informer, has so
graphically described.

Not altogether unmindful of the public censure
usually visited upon assaults like his, Mr. Reed has
endeavored, by innuendoes, to stigmatize Dr. Rush
as the persecutor of his grandfather, and to fasten
upon him the authorship of the " Brutus" queries and
of the charges in the Cadwalader pamphlet; but, he
has adduced no proof either that Dr. Rush was
" Brutus," that he *commenced* the attack upon General
Reed, or that he did more than give his testimony
when summoned by a gentleman whose assertions
had been questioned. That any other member of Dr.
Rush's family ever, directly or indirectly, raised hand,
voice, or pen, against General Reed or his descendants, Mr. Reed does not even hint. His failure to
produce any such evidence, after thirty years' search
with a microscope, proves its non-existence.

The nature of Dr. Rush's connection with the
charges against General Reed will best appear in a
brief history of the controversy, divested of what, in

other cases, Mr. Reed has called "gloss"—China gloss as it will be termed, when used by him.

Rumors—many of which reached him*—had been for years circulating in Philadelphia, charging General Reed upon the authority of General Cadwalader with contemplated, and upon that of Major Lennox with consummated, treachery, during the month of December, 1776. Though, as a politician, he must have been keenly sensitive to the importance of instantly meeting them with indignant denial and overwhelming proof, General Reed never noticed them until those which rested on the authority of General Cadwalader, in the form of queries, signed "Brutus," were published in the "Independent Gazetteer" of Sept. 7, 1782. This publication, rather than General Cadwalader's frequent statements in conversation and the often repeated rumors, has been capriciously designated by Mr. Reed, the *commencement* of the attack. General Reed then, for the first time, demanded of General Cadwalader a contradiction of the report; but, having received in its stead an emphatic and unqualified confirmation, he published a pamphlet in which he joined issue with the latter on some of his statements. In March, 1783, General Cadwalader published his celebrated reply. In connection with other certificates from Thomas Pryor,

---

* "After repeated gross and illiberal attacks of every kind from *weakness to treason*, for great pains have been taken to prove me in the interests of the enemy," &c. Letter of Reed to Greene in *June*, 1781.

Alexander Hamilton, P. Dickinson, John Nixon, Jacob Rush, Joseph Ellis, Franklin Davenport, William Bradford, David Lennox, and Francis Nichols, there appeared one from Dr. Rush, in which it was stated that, whilst holding a responsible position in the army, General Reed, in conversation with him, had displayed great want of firmness, had regretted that the war was ever commenced, and had justified the conduct of those who had deserted the cause. It was in these words:—

A few days before the battle of Trenton, on the 26th of December, 1776, I rode with Mr. Reed from Bristol to headquarters near New Town. In the course of our ride, our conversation turned upon public affairs, when Mr. Reed expressed himself in the manner following.

He spoke with great respect of the bravery of the British troops, and with great contempt of the cowardice of the American, and more especially of the New England troops. So great was the terror inspired by the British soldiers into the minds of our men, that he said, when a British soldier was brought as a prisoner to our camp, our soldiers viewed him at a distance as a superior kind of being.

Upon my lamenting to him the supposed defection of Mr. Dickinson, who it was unjustly said, had deserted his country, he used the following words: "Damn him—I wish the devil had him, when he wrote the Farmer's letters. He has begun an opposition to Great Britain which we have not strength to finish."

Upon my lamenting that a gentleman of his acquaintance had submitted to the enemy, he said "that he had acted properly, and that a man who had a family did right to take that care of them."

The whole of his conversation upon the subject of our affairs indicated a great despair of the American cause.

Upon my going to Baltimore, to take my seat in Congress, the latter end of January, I mentioned the above conversation to my brother. I likewise mentioned it to the Hon. John Adams, Esq., with whom I then lived in intimacy, a day or two after his return from Boston to Congress. I did not mention it with a view of injuring Mr. Reed, for I still respected him, especially as I then believed that the victory at Trenton had restored the tone of his mind and dissipated his fears, but to show Mr. Adams an instance of a man possessing and exercising military spirit and activity, and yet deficient in political fortitude. To which I well remember Mr. Adams replied in the following words: "The powers of the human mind are combined together in an infinite variety of ways."

BENJAMIN RUSH.

PHILADELPHIA, March 3, 1783.

General Cadwalader charged General Reed with a rapidly forming intention to imitate the treachery which, in the conversation with Dr. Rush, had been merely justified. He said:—

I had occasion to speak with you a few days before the intended attack on the 26th December, 1776, and requested you to retire with me to a private room at my quarters; the business related to intelligence; a general conversation, however, soon took place, concerning the state of public affairs; and after running over a number of topics—in an agony of mind, and despair strongly expressed in your countenance and tone of voice, you spoke your apprehensions concerning the event of the contest—that our affairs looked very desperate, and we were only making a sacrifice of ourselves; that the time of General Howe's offering pardon and protection to persons who should come in before the 1st January, 1777, was nearly expired, and that Galloway, the Allens, and others, had gone over, and availed themselves of that pardon and protection, offered by the said proclamation; that you had a family, and ought to take care of them, and that you did not understand following the wretched remains (or remnants) of a broken army; that your brother (then a colonel or lieutenant-colonel of militia—but you say of the five months' men, which is not material) was then at Burlington, with his family; and that you had advised him to remain there, and, if the enemy took possession of the town, to take a protection and swear allegiance; and in doing so he would be perfectly justifiable.

This was the substance, and I think nearly the very words; but that "*you did not understand following the wretched remains (or remnants) of a broken army,*" I perfectly remember to be the *very words* you expressed.

Mr. Philemon Dickinson said:—

HERMITAGE, 5th October, 1782.

DEAR GENERAL,—In the winter of 1776, after we had crossed the Delaware, General Reed, in conversation with me, said that he and several others of my friends were surprised at seeing me there. I told him I did not understand such a conversation; that as I had engaged in the cause from principle, I was determined to share the fate of my country; to which he made no reply, and the conversation ended. As I had the honor of commanding the militia of New Jersey, both duty and inclination led me to use every exertion in support of a cause I had engaged in from the purest motives. I was really much surprised at General Reed's manner, considering the station he then acted in, and his reputation as a patriot; but I considered it as the effect of despondency, from the then gloomy prospect of our affairs.

This I mentioned to several of my friends at the time, who all viewed it in the same point of light.

I am, dear General, yours,

P. DICKINSON.

GENERAL CADWALADER.

Mr. John Nixon said:—

I do hereby certify that, in December, 1776, while the militia lay at Bristol, General Reed, to the best of my recollection and belief, upon my inquiring the news, and what he thought of our affairs in general, said that appearances were very gloomy and unfavorable; that he was fearful *or* apprehensive the business was nearly settled, *or* the game almost up, or words to the same effect. That these sentiments appeared to me very extraordinary and dangerous, as I conceived they would, at *that time*, have a very bad tendency, if publicly known to be the sentiments of General Reed, who then held an appointment in the army of the first consequence.

JOHN NIXON.

PHILADELPHIA, March 12, 1783.

Col. Joseph Ellis said:—

Joseph Ellis, a colonel of militia, in the county of Gloucester, and State of New Jersey, doth hereby certify that, upon the retreat of a body of militia from before Count Donop, in the neighborhood of Mount Holly, in Burlington County, in the month of December, 1776, he met with Charles Pettit, Esq., *then Secretary of the said State;* that a conversation ensued between them respecting the situation of the public dispute at that period; that Mr. Pettit, in said conversation, representing that our affairs were desperate, Col. Ellis endeavored to dissuade him from such an opinion, when Mr. Pettit replied, "What hurts me more than all is, my brother-in-law, General Reed, has (or I believe he has) given up the contest." That a good deal more passed between Mr. Pettit and Col. Ellis during the said conversation, but omitted here, as being thought unnecessary.

JOSEPH ELLIS.

WOODBURY, March 9, 1783.

Mr. William Bradford said:—

These are to certify that, in December, 1776, and January, 1777, I, the subscriber, was major of the second battalion of Philadelphia militia, whereof John Bayard was colonel, and then lay at Bristol, and part of the time opposite Trenton, on the Pennsylvania side. That while we lay at Bristol, Joseph Reed, Esq., joined us; that during his being there and near Trenton, he often went out for intelligence, as Col. Bayard told me, over to Burlington, in which place the enemy frequently were; that being absent frequently all day and all night, I as frequently inquired what could become of Gen. Reed. Col. Bayard often answered me, he feared he had left us, and gone over to the enemy. One time in particular, being absent two days and two nights, if not three nights, Col. Bayard came to me with great concern, and said he was fully persuaded Gen. Reed was gone to join the enemy and make his peace. I asked him how he could possibly think so of a man who had taken so early a part, and had acted steadily. He replied, he was persuaded it was so; for he knew the General thought it was all over, and that we could not stand against the enemy; and at the same time wept much. I endeavored all I could to drive such notions from him, but he was so fully persuaded that he had left us, and gone over to the enemy, that arguing about the matter was only loss of time; Col. Bayard often making mention that he knew his sentiments much better than I did. After being absent two or three nights, Gen. Reed returned, and I never saw more joy expressed than was by Col. Bayard; he declaring to me that he was glad Gen. Reed was returned, for he was fully convinced in his own mind, that he was gone over to the enemy.

WILLIAM BRADFORD.

Manor of Moreland, Philadelphia County, March 15, 1783.

Major David Lennox said :—

Having been called on by General Cadwalader respecting a report which has been propagated concerning Mr. Joseph Reed—I declare on my honor the circumstances are as follows. In the spring of 1780 I obtained permission for an interview with my brother at Elizabethtown. In the course of conversation, one day, he happened to mention that there were men among us, who held the first offices, who applied for protection from the British while they lay in New Jersey. I was alarmed at this assertion, and insisted on knowing who they were:—He said that when the British army lay in Jersey, in 1776, Count Donop commanded at Bordentown; that he was often at that officer's quarters, and possessed some degree of his confidence; that one day *an inhabitant came into their lines, with an application from Mr. Joseph Reed, the purport of which was, to know whether he could have protection for himself and his property* (there was another person included in the *application* whose *name* it is not necessary here to mention). The man was immediately ordered for execution, but it was prevented by the interposition of my brother and some other persons, who had formerly known him. Perhaps Mr. Reed and his friends may say that Count Donop would not have ordered the man executed, had he not thought he came for intelligence. No doubt that officer would have justified his conduct by putting upon the footing of a spy, but why was another person included in the application, and one who was not looked on as a trifling character? His name I will mention to any one who will apply to me. However, my brother said the man who was sent with the application was a poor peasant, and the most unfit person in the world to send for intelligence; this argument was what had weight with Count Donop, and which saved his life. These circumstances being mentioned by a brother, and which he declared to be true, naturally produced an alteration in my sentiments of Mr. Reed; for, previous to this, there were few men of whom I entertained so high an opinion. On my return to Philadelphia, I made no secret of what I heard; indeed, I thought it my duty to mention it publicly, that it might prevent further power being put into the hands of a man who might make a bad use of it. The report circulated daily, and I was often called on to mention the circumstances, which I always did, and which I should have done to Mr. Reed, had he applied to me. I remember, among the number who came to me was Major Thomas Moore, who said he intended to inform Mr. Reed; but whether he did or not, I cannot pretend to say.

There is another thing I wish to mention. My brother came into the river in a flag of truce, on special application of our commissary of prisoners, to take a number of prisoners who were exchanged, to save us the expense and trouble of sending them by land; this was in the month of May, 1781. He was detained, about nine miles below the city, upwards of four weeks, and never permitted to visit it, although application was made for that purpose by several captains of vessels, who had been prisoners, and to whom he had rendered civilities. I declined making application myself, as I supposed my being in the service from the commencement of the war, and having endured a rigorous confinement for eighteen months, in the worst of times, to have been sufficient to have obtained permission for a brother to have been in my house, in preference to a cabin in a small vessel in a river; however, I endeavored to make his situation as agreeable as possible, by visiting him often, and by taking my friends with me. I REMEMBER Col. Francis Nichols went with me, one day, to whom my brother mentioned Mr. Reed's intended desertion, and who, I doubt not, will acknowledge it, on any person's applying to him; he is at present in Virginia, but is expected in town in a few days.

DAVID LENNOX.

Mr. Francis Nichols said:—

Having been called upon, by General Cadwalader, to certify, so far as my knowledge extends, as to the matter hereinafter mentioned, I do declare that in the spring of the year 1781 I went with Major Lennox, of this city, on board of a flag of truce vessel, then lying in the river Delaware, where she had arrived from New York, and heard Mr. Robert Lennox, deputy commissary of prisoners under the British king, say that in the year of 1776 a person had arrived at Count Donop's quarters, near Bordentown, in New Jersey, who told the Count that he had been sent to him by General Reed and another person, whose name I do not think necessary to mention, to procure a protection for them; that the Count refused to grant them a protection in that manner, and was about to treat the person who had applied to him as a spy, but was prevented by the entreaties of the said Robert Lennox and some other gentlemen.

FRANCIS NICHOLS.

PHILADELPHIA, 17th March, 1783.

This mass of testimony, more damning than that of Dr. Rush, shows that he was not the "chief witness" against General Reed, and that he was not exceptionally active in the last stages of the controversy. What was his connection with its earlier ones?

Mr. Reed wishes his readers to infer, what he does not dare positively to assert, that Dr. Rush was "Brutus." As an unequalled specimen of literary thimble-rigging, three of his paragraphs are given, in which, with the lightning's rapidity, he makes Rush disappear under Brutus, Brutus under Rush, and then both to disappear, widely separated, forever.

" The newspapers of the date attribute it to Dr. Benjamin Rush, and, as he subsequently made himself a chief witness in support of the accusations against Mr. Reed, was bitterly hostile to him, and was addicted to this mode of secret assault; there is reason for attributing to his busy pen the initiation of this wretched controversy"—a controversy which maintains its character in Mr. Reed's hands. " But, *if* Dr. Rush be ' Brutus,' and this, on the evidence, is my belief; *if* it is he who started this wretched controversy, then his relation to the whole affair is widely different." " *If* Dr. Rush was ' Brutus,' it is very clear that, so far as he is concerned, the allegata and probata strangely conflict; for the ' Queries of Brutus' and the certificate of Rush do not refer to the same facts, or similar facts, in any single point of resemblance. Why, one may ask, this discrepancy, the agents or authors being the same? Was it that, one accusation being made anonymously, another was purposely held back to be used as a sort of corroboration? Why was it, ' Brutus' being Rush, that the queries referred to what Mr. Reed is reported to have said to 'the commanding officer at Bristol,' and not at all to what he said to the companion of the ride to Newtown? If Dr. Rush was ' Brutus,' or, indeed, if he were only ' Brutus'' chief authority," &c. &c. " *Brutus never came from his ambush.*"

Did it never occur to Mr. Reed whilst shaping and reshaping his query, " Why this discrepancy, the agents and authors being the same," that the riddle he propounded was akin to the celebrated problem in specific gravity with which King Charles so long puzzled the savans, and that it was only upon his assumption of what did not exist, that any question arose? Fascinating as the athletic amusement of setting up and knocking down ten-pins may be, to one who has never previously indulged in other exercise than the turning of political somersets, it is astonishing to see such ardor in the game as confuses the player's recollection of the fact that the pins over whose downfall he rejoices were never in jeopardy until placed there at his own instance.

As 'Brutus' never alluded to the conversation with Dr. Rush, but quoted from that with General Cadwalader, which was matter of public notoriety, why identify him with the former rather than with one of that host of enemies of whose numbers General Reed so bitterly complained? Because he was a "chief witness?" It has been shown that he was not. Because he was "bitterly hostile?" So were hundreds of General Reed's cotemporaries. Because "he was addicted to this mode of secret assault?" No such habit has been proven.

In Mr. Reed's abuse of Dr. Rush he has acted in anything but the Biblical spirit, on the Biblical maxim, "It is more blessed to give than to receive;" but he has attacked with such bitter hostility and with so little regard to success in his avowed design, that his course must be attributed to some cause other than the one he has assigned. Must we explain it by quoting from Mr. Reed in his own condemnation?

"A calumny may have been buried in obscurity for centuries and millenaries, and at length some *literary truffle dog* will hunt it out." Is it to the instincts of "the literary truffle dog," whose Roman nose, more Roman at least than his virtue, lacks the trueness of scent which characterizes the convoluted nostrils of his prototype, that we must attribute this exhuming of what, even with "China gloss," hardly rises to the dignity of calumny?

Or, must we attribute it to the spirit of the next of kin to the literary truffle dog—the dog in the manger—to Mr. Reed's determination, his hoisting process having failed, to still place General Reed on a level with the accredited patriots of the Revolution, by dragging the latter down? Did he hope, in his ancestor's words, provided he could afterwards surreptitiously trim off its blackened wick, and supply a more modern illuminating material from his own manufactory, that the ancestral "candle would shine better if every other was extinguished?"

Having thus shown the animus and unprovoked nature of Mr. Reed's attack on Dr. Rush, it remains to show its want of foundation, which will be done by attempting to demonstrate the following propositions, involving necessarily an *incidental* consideration of many of the specifications of the first of the above counts. The peculiar line of defence, an attack on the character of the witnesses for the commonwealth, which alone seemed open to Mr. Reed after eighty-four years' deliberation, is one only adopted in very desperate cases, inasmuch as the citadel is left entirely unprotected, if the assaulting column into which has been drafted the whole garrison, is once beaten. Though fire-ships rarely destroy the vessels against which they are launched, they are always themselves consumed.

FIRST. Dr. Rush's credibility has been impeached

without any regard to the rules of evidence, and without any proofs or even specifications of a want of *veracity.*

SECOND. His testimony is outside the range of *Mr. Reed's* impeachment, inasmuch as it was given before the "passions were involved," on whose existence the latter predicated his aspersions.

THIRD. There is nothing derogatory to Dr. Rush's character in any particular, in the *matter* of Mr. Reed's specifications, though the collocation and manner of statement are offensive.

FOURTH. His testimony is corroborated by its own intrinsic evidence and by extrinsic proofs.

FIFTH. It has never been directly contradicted; nor has the corroborative testimony *relied on* ever been assailed, otherwise than by the unsupported denial of General Reed, who was not only disqualified from testifying by his interest in the result, but was also, in any such matter, "utterly unworthy of belief."

SIXTH. Mr. Reed's aspersions are utterly at variance with cotemporaneous opinions of Dr. Rush.

FIRST. Dr. Rush's testimony is entitled to no weight if Mr. Reed's assertion that he was "utterly unworthy of belief" is correct. This must be established, however, in accordance with widely adopted, long-established rules—by the evidence of those who, knowing the character of the impeached witness for veracity amongst his neighbors and acquaintances, from the badness of his *reputation*, in this respect, would not believe him on his oath. Under the avalanche with which he would have been overwhelmed from tradition, eulogiums, biographies, encyclopædias, and histories, Mr. Reed does not venture an assertion that Dr. Rush's *reputation* for veracity, amongst those who knew him, was bad. Nor is the utterance of a single falsehood proven; nor any act involving a deficiency in truthfulness.

Whence then does he draw the conclusion that Dr. Rush was utterly unworthy of belief? From his failure to appreciate Washington's military ability? From his letter to Richard H. Lee manifesting a desire to punish the Tories who had maltreated his father-in-law? From a surgical statement as to the immediate cause of General Mercer's death? From the charges of mal-practices and neglect, whose truth Mr. Reed does not question, made to Dr. Shippen's official chief? From his slight participation in the politics of Pennsylvania, of whose demoralizing effects none better than Mr. Reed can speak? From Mr. Jacob Rush's disappointment in obtaining an office of which he was little desirous? These are all the specifications which have been accumulated in a thirty years' apprenticeship to the trade of the literary scavenger, and as they do not sustain the charge, it falls. No greater tribute to Dr. Rush could be paid by the most lavish praise, than by this failure of Mr. Reed, who lacked neither time, spleen, nor ability, and whom no regard for the living or dead restrained; nor could a more damaging admission of the hopelessness of General Reed's cause be made, than by the paltriness of the expedients to which his able advocate has felt obliged to resort.

SECONDLY. Dr. Rush's testimony stands unimpeached by *Mr. Reed*, if it can be shown that it was given before his "passions were involved."

In January, 1777, when no such passions could have been subserved by General Reed's defamation, as he had not yet deserted the ranks of the Anti-Constitutionalists, this testimony, as subsequently repeated, was first given. So Dr. and Judge Rush assert, in their respective certificates of 3d March, 1783, and the former refers to Mr. John Adams, whose comments are quoted, as one who heard it. Every man, from his own personal experience, estimates the extent to which falsehood is induced by private and political passions. If Mr. Reed believes that these passions would instigate two persons, not hopelessly depraved, to the deliberate utterance of false, malicious, easily detected untruths, he cannot be convinced that these confirmatory conversations were ever held; but the more fortunate experience of others will, it is thought, render an appeal to their beliefs much more successful. A single line of denial from Mr. Adams, too, who was never involved in Pennsylvania affairs, and whose politics were widely different from those of Dr. Rush, at any time during the succeeding thirty years, would have convicted the latter of a gross falsehood. *This denial was never obtained.* Nor would Dr. Rush, if the conversation was imaginary, have assigned to Mr. Adams a part in it which could have been so much more safely filled by any one of the hosts whom the havoc of war had swept into the grave.

In this connection, in illustration of the danger of touching pitch, occurs one of the too numerous instances of the "vice" of mis-quotation which, "seen too oft" by Mr. Reed in his researches in Bancroft, he has at last himself "embraced." Dr. Rush never said of the effect of General Reed's conversation that it "did not *diminish* his respect," but merely that for other qualities he "still respected" the latter.

The THIRD proposition will be demonstrated by a detailed examination of the different specifications of Mr. Reed's charges, in their order.

He has painted a portrait and labelled it "Dr.

Rush," the lineaments of which are those of a "re-vengeful, exasperated man," a "tattler," a "fisher in troubled waters," a "scoffer at the grave of the dead," a monger in "scandal," a "writer of anony-mous defamation," "a busy, restless, *indirect* man, emphatically a *man of animosities*," a man "utterly unworthy of belief as a witness for anything in which his passions were involved," in the drawing of which, inasmuch as it cannot be identified with its ostensi-ble original, he must have imitated the practice of those artists who, lacking the means or the inclina-tion to procure suitable models, delineate the human figure after intense examination of a mirror hung before themselves.

Safe in the knowledge that on behalf of the dead no action for slander will lie, Mr. Reed gleefully re-fers to the "fearful retribution" Dr. Rush experienced in the "fierce invectives" of Wm. Cobbett, "the Por-cupine;" but, he fails to narrate the sequel, of a refusal of the satisfaction then usually accorded by gentlemen, and an award, by a jury, of damages in the amount of $5000, subsequently apportioned by Dr. Rush amongst the poor.

After having admitted that he was utterly unfit to judge of Dr. Rush's professional abilities, Mr. Reed sneers at him for recording "in his dreary Note-book that General Mercer did not die of his wounds, but from natural causes." A similar statement is to be found in well-authenticated cotemporaneous diaries, and Mr. Reed ought not to expect that any one, after a lapse of ninety years, will prefer his opinion on a medical question to that of a competent physician, at the time.

Mr. Adams' letter to Dr. Rush of the 18th April, 1790, quoted as if written in complaint of the latter, was penned in a far different spirit, and breathes sentiments of the warmest friendship and most cordial esteem.

Without any pretence that his charges were malicious or unfounded, Dr. Rush is sneered at as still engaged in the " work of secret (?) accusation which never seemed to intermit," because, to the Commander-in-Chief, he preferred charges against Dr. Shippen of mal-practices and neglect, in the office of Director-General of the Middle Department, which had come under his official notice whilst he was himself Surgeon-General of military hospitals for the same department.

Must we accuse Judge Rush of the invention of one, and Dr. Rush of the invention, with every minuteness of detail, of three, imaginary conversations, because of General Reed's ill-mannered response to the former's intimation, through a third party, " not wishing to make a point of it or to urge it, that he would be willing to accept the Attorney-Generalship in case of an appointment"? If it must be inferred from Mr. Reed's remarks that pique or revenge would carry him thus far, and he will not claim to be judged by a more favorable standard than that by which he judges, it is much to be regretted, that in taking to *his quills* in imitation of the "Porcupine" he so much admires, he has also fallen into the error into which its fury leads it, whilst emptying its quiver, of helplessly exposing to its assailants its weakest parts.

The matter, however, upon which Mr. Reed most relies as demonstrating Dr. Rush's want of credibility, is his failure, during the early years of the Revolution, to appreciate Washington's military abilities. Dr. Rush's unflinching determination to maintain to the end the struggle for his country's independence is admitted. In common, however, with John and Samuel Adams, and many other leading men of the time, during those gloomy and disastrous years in which Washington's great talents were obscured, he felt that intense, unselfish craving for success, through change, which every loyal man experienced with such fearful earnestness during the stagnant years of the recent Rebellion. Having irretrievably committed himself by signing the Declaration of Independence, Dr. Rush, though he felt no inclination to retrace his steps or to temporize, was anxious beyond measure to see at the head of the army one who could chain Victory to its banners. Did an error of judgment under such circumstances affect his veracity?

Early in 1778, Dr. Rush addressed to Patrick Henry a letter, not signed, in which were these words:—

"The Northern Army has shown us what Americans are capable of doing with a General at their head. The spirit of the Southern Army is no ways inferior to the spirit of the Northern. A Gates, a Lee, or a Conway, would in a few weeks render them an irresistible body of men. The last of the above officers has accepted the new office of Inspector-General of our army, in order to reform abuses; but the remedy is only a palliative one. In one of his letters to a friend he says, 'A great and good God hath decreed America to be free, or the General and weak counsellors would have ruined her long ago.'" Of the weakness of some of Washington's counsellors and of the abuses in the army, General Reed himself, in his correspondence, had frequently complained. No desire to "stab in the dark" is displayed in any part of this letter, but merely the wish to "awaken, enlighten, and alarm our country." Dr. Rush's pen was restrained by no profuse oral and written protestations of respect for Washington's military abilities, by no friendly relation as custodian of his secrets, and by no membership in his military family. That Washington was deeply wounded by this as by all the other evidence of a non-appreciation by the public of his labors, is beyond doubt, and, thus wounded, he said, "The anonymous letter with which you were pleased to favor me, was written by Dr. Rush, so far as I can judge from a similitude of hands. This man has been elaborate and studied in his professions of regard for me; and long since the letter to you." There was of course in Dr. Rush's professions of regard for Washington as a man—professions in which few failed to unite—nothing inconsistent with the distrust of his military capacity expressed to Mr. Henry.

This letter was not anonymous in a censurable sense. Its writer, whilst entertaining no wish to withhold its authorship from his correspondent, might well take precautions, whilst communications were so uncertain, to conceal it from strangers into whose hands it might fall.* For the purpose of giving the clew to Mr. Henry, the letter, though written from Yorktown, announced that it was from one of his "*Philadelphia* friends," and directed attention to the handwriting, which was so marked that Washington, who had no better reason for recognizing it than Mr. Henry, had no difficulty in its identification.

If Dr. Rush's mere *repetition* of the anecdote of Washington's interview with the clergy is open to the charge of "scoffing at the dead" (for the portions of the Ana *not quoted* show that the comment

* The reader is referred to Peter Force's Archives, 4th series, vol. i. pp. 892 and 963, for instances of a like precaution adopted by General Joseph Reed in two letters to Josiah Quincy, Jr.

objected to was not his, but Mr. Asa Green's), then is Jefferson, who reduced it to writing, equally guilty, and Mr. Reed, who so long after it was forgotten has resurrected it, more guilty than all.

FOURTH. The testimony of Dr. Rush bears upon it the sterling mark of truth. Its intrinsic evidence is strongly in its favor. All the details are given clearly and naturally, without any of that haziness of statement which characterizes a garbled story. General Reed's subsequently published correspondence, too, evinces the same strong dislike of New England troops to which Dr. Rush testifies.

As to the extrinsic proof.

General Reed's previous history induces a more ready belief that the words reported by Dr. Rush were really uttered by him, than if they were charged against one who had been an early and uncompromising advocate of separation from Great Britain. Almost against his will, as will be shown, he became a participant in the war, an officer of the army, and a supporter of the Declaration of Independence.

He conducted a unilateral correspondence with Lord Dartmouth, the British Secretary of State for the Colonies, in which, for upwards of eighteen months, he kept the latter fully informed of the progress of disaffection in America. About two months before the battle of Lexington, viz., on the 10th day of February, 1775, amidst the din of preparation for the then almost inevitable conflict, though condemning the British taxation and coercion measures, to which he was, of course, always opposed, he wrote:—

"If the confidence my fellow-citizens repose in me, and which has led to more activity than I wished or intended, have not rendered me unworthy of your Lordship's further notice, (!) I shall cheerfully continue my communications; and do with .sincerity declare that my present or any future influence shall be faithfully exerted, not to widen the present breach, but to dispose the minds of those around me to such measures as may be consistent with the dignity and interest of the Mother Country and the safety of this. I hope and believe I have already been instrumental in guarding this city and province from measures which had an irritating tendency; and while I am thus employed, I trust I am acting the part of a good subject and citizen." In the Provincial Convention which had just met, "it was intended to take some steps towards arming and disciplining the province, a measure which I opposed both publicly and privately."

To his wife, in a letter announcing and half apologizing for his sudden acceptance of the position of Adjutant-General to which he had been elected on the 5th day of June, 1776, he said:—

"I have been much induced to this measure by observing that this Province will be a great scene of party and contention this summer. The courts are stopped, consequently no business done in my profession, and at all events my time so engrossed that I have not a moment to devote to keeping up my stock or adding to my law knowledge. The appointments of the office are equal to £700 per annum, which will help to support us till these calamitous times are at an end. Besides, this post is honorable, and if the issue is favorable to America, must put me on a respectable scale.* Should it be otherwise, I have done enough to expose myself to ruin."

To his brother-in-law, Mr. De Berdt, 20th February, 1777, he said :—

"I then waited impatiently for a public disclosure of some terms or propositions from Lord Howe and his brother. If they had been such as would give my country any (!) security against the unlimited powers of your Parliament to deprive us of our property at any time and in what proportions they pleased, I should have applied myself most earnestly to have brought about an accommodation, and if those in power had wantonly or wickedly rejected the proposition, I should have retired from the army to a private and obscure station."

To Robert Morris, after the Declaration of Independence, in referring to Lord Howe's Commission, he said :—

"I fear the die is irrevocably cast, and that we must play the game, however doubtful or desperate. My principles have been much misunderstood if they were supposed to militate against reconciliation."

These sentiments were so well known to the enemies of his country, that in 1776, and again in 1778, he was applied to by the British Commissioners as

---

* "Mammon, the least erected spirit that fell
  From Heaven; for even in Heaven his looks and thoughts
  Were always downward bent, admiring more
  The riches of Heaven's pavement, trodden gold,
  Than aught divine or holy else enjoyed
  In vision beatific."

being one most likely to lend a willing ear to propositions of compromise.

Again, in corroboration. Though the occurrence of a conversation can only be directly proven by those who overheard it, evidence of other conversations of a like nature by the same person at about the same time, and of a general frame of mind in harmony with that indicated by it, is strongly persuasive, if not in exact accordance with strict legal rules.

By Mr. Charles Pettit, his brother-in-law, and most intimate friend, who subsequently became one of his executors, General Reed was believed to have "given up the contest." Mr. Reed condemns, as "hearsay gossip," the testimony of Col. Ellis and Mr. Davenport; but, in an investigation like this, such evidence is free from the objection which so justly excludes "hearsay" from the courts, viz., the impossibility of obtaining any refutation of it before the rendering of the verdict. Wherever there was the slightest opening, as in the case of Mr. Wm. Bradford's testimony, General Reed was very prompt in procuring the denial of the person with whom any damaging conversation was alleged to have been held. His failure to obtain from Mr. Pettit, with whom he was so intimate, any such denial, is very significant. We thus, in effect, have one of his bosom friends testifying to his belief, one which without imperative cause he would have been slow to entertain and still slower to confess, that General Reed, in December, 1776, "had given up the contest."

To Mr. P. Dickinson, whom, though an officer in the militia force, no official position *compelled* to be with the army, General Reed, on "seeing him there," at a time when the exigency demanded the presence of all who could bear arms, expressed surprise.

General Cadwalader, whose veracity Mr. Reed has not openly and directly impeached, but at whom he has aimed side blows, testifies to utterances of General Reed, in December, 1776, much more censurable than those reported by Dr. Rush.

Mistakes are attributed to General Cadwalader in two minor particulars, for the purpose of discrediting the general accuracy of his memory.

The first is thus imagined by Mr. Reed :—

" Again, there is an illustration of mistaken memory, when, in reply to the statement in Mr. Reed's address, that he went to Burlington before day, but did not leave Dunk's Ferry till he saw the last man embarked, General Cadwalader in his pamphlet of 1783, said this could not be, for ' there is no circumstance better ascertained than that many of the men were not brought back till *eight o'clock* the next morning.' Writing to General Washington, on the very day (25th), Cadwalader said: ' We concluded to withdraw the troops that had passed, but could not effect it till near *four o'clock* in the morning. The whole was then ordered to march back to Bristol.' Four o'clock on Christmas morning is certainly long ' before day.' "

Though the truth or falsity of the statement made by General Cadwalader in his pamphlet was in the knowledge of hundreds of living men, no one ventured to contradict it. An announcement of a withdrawal at four o'clock appears inconsistent with the return of "many of the men" four hours later, to no one whom the recent Rebellion made familiar with the evil of "straggling from the ranks." General Reed's assertion, to which exception was taken, was, not that he had waited for the embarkation of the main body, but for that of the "*last man.*" ·

The second inaccuracy is thus manufactured:—

"The troops at Bristol crossed the Delaware on the 27th, it being supposed that Washington was still on the left bank. On landing, it was ascertained that he had re-crossed, and it became a question what should be done by the force below. Writing of this, in 1783, General Cadwalader, in his pamphlet says, that on the receipt of news that Washington had re-crossed, 'Colonel Hitchcock proposed returning to Bristol. *I instantly declared my determination against it,* and recommended an attack on Mount Holly, as, from the information we had of the force there, we might easily carry it.' There now lies before me a certified copy from the State Department of a letter from General Cadwalader to Washington, dated on the very day of the occurrence, 'Burlington, ten o'clock, 27th,' in which he says: * * * '*I thought it most prudent to retreat,* but Colonel Reed was of opinion that we might safely proceed to Burlington, and recommended it warmly,'" &c.

The implied conflict of statements is produced by Mr. Reed's closing General Cadwalader's sentence, which, in full, reads: "Col. Hitchcock proposed returning to Bristol. I instantly declared my determination against it, and recommended an attack on Mount Holly, as, from the information of the force there, we might easily carry it, *and should then have a retreat open towards Philadelphia, if necessary,*" with the words "might easily carry it." He quotes so as to make it appear that but two courses of action were discussed, a retreat and an advance, whilst, in reality, there was a medium course, combining both, viz: a march to Mount Holly, which General Cadwalader, who from the outset opposed the others, strongly favored.

A further attempt is made to refute General Cadwalader's assertion that General Reed had informed him he had advised his brother to remain at Burlington, "and *if the enemy took possession of the town, to take* protection," by means of an affidavit by Mr. Bowes Reed that he was never advised to "*seek*" protection, which besides being evasive, is wholly irrelevant to the real issue, General Reed's report to General Cadwalader of the advice he had given.

In imitation of the military tactics of the Celestials, with whom dragons and gongs are esteemed more potent than powder and ball, the ghost of "party rage" is conjured from its grave by the *modern Witch of Endor.* Again, however, it is found that the testimony, first given in the Campaign of 1777, antedates the era of party passions. Alexander Hamilton proves this, and Mr. Reed can only evade his blow by suppressing his exact words and erroneously stating their substance. He says:—

" There is not a trace of General Cadwalader having breathed this accusation until the Treason trials of 1778. The only attempt to show that he ever whispered it before, is in Col. Hamilton's letter of the 14th of March, 1783, in which he says that after an effort of memory '*he thinks*' the matter was mentioned to him some time in the Campaign of 1777, and with great caution he adds: 'It is the part of candour to observe that I am not able to distinguish with certainty whether the recollection I have of these words arises from the strong impression made by your declaration at the time or from having heard them more than once repeated within a year past.' "

The extent of Mr. Reed's misquotations will appear upon reading Col. Hamilton's own language :—

PHILADELPHIA, 14th March, 1783.

DEAR SIR: Though disagreeable to appear in any manner in a personal dispute; yet I cannot, in justice to you, refuse to comply with the request contained in your note. I have delayed answering it, to endeavor to recollect, with more precision, the time, place, and circumstances of the conversation to which you allude. I cannot, however, remember with certainty more than this; that some time in the campaign of seventy-seven, at headquarters in this State, you mentioned to me and some other gentlemen of General Washington's family, in a confidential way, that at some period in seventy-six, I think after the American army crossed the Delaware in its retreat, Mr. Reed had spoken to you in terms of great despondency respecting American affairs, and had intimated that he thought it time for gentlemen to take care of themselves, and that it was unwise any longer to follow the fortunes of a ruined cause, or something of a similar import. It runs in my mind that the expressions you declared to have been made use of by Mr. Reed were, that he thought he ought no longer to " risque his life and fortune with the shattered remains of a broken army;" but it is the part of candor to observe that I am not able to distinguish with certainty whether the recollection I have of these words arises from the strong impression made by your declaration at the time, or from having heard them more than once repeated within a year past.

I am, dear sir, with great esteem,

Your obedient servant,

To GENERAL CADWALADER.   A. HAMILTON.

Col. Hamilton "*remembers with certainty*" that some time in the campaign of 1777 the matter was mentioned to him, and also that the substance of the conversation was that first given by him. The precise phraseology, as stated in the last sentence, was alone a little doubtful.

Mr. Reed labors to show such treatment of his ancestor by General Cadwalader as was inconsistent with a belief of his own charges. The latter's answer to a somewhat similar argument by General Reed, needs no supplement now.

FIFTH. In discussing the weight to be attached to General Reed's denial of a portion of the charges against him, it will be shown that he was guilty of many falsehoods, and that, therefore, where his own interests were involved, he was "utterly unworthy of belief." After having ignored every rule of evidence himself, Mr. Reed cannot now object, in resisting his *guerilla* attack, to this irregular mode of impeaching the credibility of one not legally admissible as a witness.

General Reed's mendacity will not be proven by any quotations from the discredited and discreditable "Valley Forge" letters. Two publications alone will be used, the one known as the "Cadwalader Pamphlet," the other a work whose descriptions of its hero's great deeds—deeds which may be eulogized in the words by which faith has been defined*—are made *life-like* by a recital which consumes fully as much time in the telling as was required for the doing, and of which may be asserted what was said of the picturesque style of Macaulay's History, and with more truth, "It reads like a romance"—the "Life and Correspondence of General Reed by his Grandson." Before entering the pasteboard palace in which Mr. Reed had enshrined his idol, it was found necessary to rearrange a little the cards with which he had constructed it; but then, the privilege of "cutting" after those very adroit in shuffling, must be exercised in most games of cards.

Though a careful sifting of the evidence with which Mr. Reed has sought to prove the alleged offer of £10,000 sterling as a bribe,† leads to an almost inevitable conviction of the truth of Gov. Johnstone's emphatic denial of it, especially in view of his candid admission, whilst disclaiming their use with General Reed, that he had "used other means besides per-

---

* Hebrews xi. 1.   † Life of Reed, vol. i. pp. 381 to 394.

suasions" in some cases, yet, as Mrs. Ferguson, without authority, *may* have offered the bribe, and *may* have asserted to the latter that such authority had been given her, his assertions in this matter will not be discussed under the present head.

A passing allusion alone will be made both to General Reed's misrepresentation, during the correspondence antecedent to the pamphlets, of Mr. Ingersoll's report of General Cadwalader's remarks as to the time he was expecting to leave Philadelphia; and to his assertions in his Address to the Public that he had "left a lucrative practice and fair prospects to impoverish himself in their service," though, as he admitted in a private letter to his brother-in-law, "the war being brought to our own doors" * * * "banished every idea of law, so that the profession for which it had been my earliest study to qualify myself is become entirely useless," and though he entered the public service, partly, at least, as the letter to his wife, already quoted, shows, because "its appointments, equal to £700 per annum," would help to support his family.

General Reed, however, was accused by General Cadwalader in these words of what he never ventured to deny :—

"And further (with respect to your veracity), if any other instance is necessary, let me add one which happened at camp (at head-quarters) in the year 1777, soon after the battle of Germantown, when in my

hearing, and in the presence of three officers of the
first rank in the army, you was charged to your face
with a falsehood, and which was fully proved the next
day by the general officer who made the charge."

The transaction, however, which put upon General
Reed an ineffaceable brand, is the one so well known
that its narration is justly chargeable by his grandson, who seems strangely insensible to the strong condemnation which lies therein, with the accusation of
being "stale."*   It grew out of that desire to be on
the winning side, unlike Dr. Rush's sympathy, which
Mr. Reed has noticed, with those "under a cloud,"
which prompted General Reed, after the brilliant victory at Saratoga, whilst for Washington's military
capacity, to Washington himself, he was still loud
in his protestation of respect, to flatter General Gates
by saying, "This army, notwithstanding the efforts
of our amiable (!) chief, has as yet gained no laurels.
I perfectly agree with the sentiment which leads to
request your assistance."

On the 16th day of November, 1776, Fort Washington, the policy of whose retention had been warmly
canvassed in the American councils, with its whole

---

* After all the following matter connected with the Lee-Reed correspondence was in type, the writer, who had never before seen Mr. John C.
Hamilton's history, though it had been referred to by Mr. Reed, found that
the whole subject had been therein considered in a manner so similar that
his own will only be regarded as a quotation from Mr. Hamilton. Its
appositeness, however, is none the less, and it is therefore retained.

garrison, was captured by the British. Washington's conduct in the matter was by some severely censured, but, conceiving that under the instructions of Congress he had not been permitted to evacuate it, such unfavorable criticisms pained him exceedingly. General Charles Lee, who had formerly held high rank in the British army, was at the time looked upon as the probable successor of Washington, against whom he was intriguing. General Reed was then Washington's Adjutant-General, professed himself his bosom friend and warmest admirer, was thoroughly acquainted with his views and feelings, and was intrusted with his confidence. To Lee, then in command of the rear-guard on the east side of the Hudson, whilst basking in the sunshine of his Chief's favor, General Reed addressed the following letter. The italics in this and the subsequent ones are the writer's.

HACKINSAC, November 21, 1776.

DEAR GENERAL,—The letter you will receive with this contains my sentiments with respect to your present situation. But besides this I have some additional reasons for wishing most earnestly to have you where the principal scene of action is laid. *I do not mean to flatter or praise you at the expense of any other, but I confess I do think it is entirely owing to you that this army, and the liberties of America, so far as they are dependent on it, are not totally cut off. You have decision, a quality often wanted in minds otherwise valuable, and I ascribe to this our escape from York Island, from Kingsbridge, and the Plains, and have no doubt, had you been here, the garrison of Mount Washington would now have composed part of this army.* All these circumstances considered, I confess I ardently wish to see you removed where I think there will be little call for your judgment and experience to the place where they are likely to be so necessary, nor am I singular in my opinion. Every gentleman of the family, the officers and soldiers generally, have a confidence in you—the enemy constantly inquire where you are, and seem to be less confident when you are present. Colonel Cadwalader, through a special indulgence, on account of some civilities shown by his family to General Prescott, has been liberated from New York without a parole. He informs me that the enemy have a southern expedition in view—*that they hold us very cheap in consequence of the late affair at Fort Washington, where both the plan of defence and execution were contemptible. If a real defence of the lines was intended, the number of troops was too few—if the fort only, the garrison was too numerous by half. General Washington's own judgment, seconded by representations by us, would, I believe, have saved the men and their arms, but unluckily General Greene's judgment was adverse. This kept the General's mind in a state of suspense till the blow was struck. Oh! General, an indecisive mind is one of the greatest misfortunes that can befall an army; how often have I lamented it this campaign.* All circumstances considered, we are in a very awful and alarming situation—one that requires the utmost wisdom and firmness of mind. As soon as the season will admit, I think yourself and some others should go to Congress and form the plan of the new army, point out their defects to them, and it may possibly prevail on them to lend their whole attention to this great object, even to the exclusion of every other. If they will not or cannot do this, I fear all our exertions will be vain in this part of the world. Foreign assistance is solicited, but we cannot expect they will fight the whole battle. But artillery and artillerists must be had if possible. I intended to say more, but the express is waiting, and I must conclude with my clear and explicit opinion that *your presence is of the last importance.*

Yours, &c.

To this letter, Lee, highly delighted with such evidence of disaffection and distrust in Washington's military family, replied as follows:—

CAMP, November 24, 1776.

MY DEAR REED,—I received your most obliging, flattering letter, lament with you that fatal indecision of mind which in war is a much greater disqualification than stupidity, or even want of personal courage; accident may put a decisive blunder in the right, but eternal defeat and miscarriage must attend the man of the best parts if cursed with indecision. The General recommends in so pressing a manner as almost to amount to an order, to bring over the Continental troops under my command, which recommendation or order throws me into the greatest dilemma from several considerations. Part of the troops are so ill furnished with shoes and stockings, blankets, &c., that they must inevitably perish in this wretched weather. Part of them are to be dismissed on Saturday, and this part is the best accoutred for service. What shelter we are to find on the other side of the river is a serious consideration; but these considerations should not sway me. My reason for not having marched already is that we have just received intelligence that Rogers' Corps, the Light Horse, part of the Highlanders and another brigade lie in so exposed a situation as to give the fairest opportunity of being carried. I should have attempted it last night, but the rain was too violent, and when our pieces are wet you know our troops are "hors du combat." This night I hope will be better. If we succeed we shall be well compensated for the delay; we shall likewise be able on our return to clear the country of all the articles wanted by the enemy. In every view, therefore, the expedition must answer. I have just received a most flattering letter from Don Luis Venzaga, Governor of New Orleans. He gives me the title of "*General de los Estados Unidos Americanos*," which is a tolerable step towards declaring himself our ally in positive terms.

The substance is, that he is sensible of the vast advantages which must result from the separation to his master and nation—that he cannot positively enter into a regular system without consulting his master, but in the mean time he will render us all the service in his power. I only wait myself for this business of Rogers and company being over. I shall then fly to you; for, to confess a truth, I really think our Chief will do better with me than without me.

I am, dear Reed, yours most sincerely,

CHARLES LEE.

"This letter was forwarded to camp by express, and being supposed to relate to official business, was opened and read by Washington, Colonel Reed being absent on special duty at Burlington. It appears to have wounded him deeply." It was transmitted by Washington, with a few cold words of explanation, on the 30th of November, 1776.

Until Lee's capture induced General Reed to hope, as he admitted himself, that the former would "be sent to Europe, where, of course, there was little probability of any one obtaining it," he did not dare to assert that the former's letter was not justified by his own; but, after this event had occurred, and after several months and hosts of opportunities for oral and written explanations had passed, his appointment as a general of cavalry being then pending, he addressed Washington a letter under date of the 8th of March, 1777, in which this passage occurs:—

"I could have wished to have one hour of private conversation with you on the subject of a letter to me written by General Lee before his captivity. I deferred it in hopes of obtaining from him the letter to which his was an answer. I fear from what we hear that he will be sent to England, and of course there will be little probability of my obtaining it. While he stays in America, I cannot give up my hopes, and in the mean time *I most solemnly assure you, that you would see in it nothing inconsistent with that respect and affection which I have and ever shall bear to your person and character. My pressing him most earnestly to join you as soon as possible, and mentioning that Mount Washington was taken before any decision was had respecting it, led to expressions and an answer which must have been disapproved by you, and which I was far from expecting.* I had rather multiply instances than repeat assurances of my respect and attachment. No man in America, my dear General, more truly and ardently wishes your honor, happiness, and success, or would more exert himself to promote them. I say more upon this occasion from a probability that we shall not renew our military connexion, and therefore can have no interest than that of securing your esteem, free from all selfish principles."

On the 4th of June, 1777, Reed again addressed Washington, thus:—

"The abuse and calumny which, with equal cowardice and baseness, some persons have bestowed, would have given me little pain if I did not apprehend that it had lessened me in your friendship and esteem. In this part I confess I have received the severest wound; for I am sure you are too just and discerning to suffer the unguarded expressions of another person to obliterate the proofs I have given of a sincere disinterested attachment to your person and fame, since you first favored me with your regard. I am sensible, my dear sir, how difficult it is to regain lost friendship, but the consciousness of never having justly forfeited yours, and the hope that it may be in my power fully to convince you of it, are some consolation for an event which I never think of but with the greatest concern. In the meantime, my dear general, let me entreat of you to *judge of me by realities, not by appearances, and believe that I never entertained or expressed a sentiment incompatible with that regard I professed for your person and character,* and which, whether I shall be so happy as to possess your future good opinion or not, I shall carry to my grave with me."

Though General Reed asserts that Lee's expressions, at which Washington took offence, were in no way responsive to his own, which contained nothing "inconsistent with respect for your character," and that the mere mentioning that Mount Washington had been taken before any decision was had respecting it, led to "expressions which must have been disapproved by you, and which I was far from expecting," they were, in truth, infinitely more friendly and respectful than Reed's. Lee thinks "our chief will be better with me than without me," laments that "fatal indecision of mind which in war is a much greater disqualification than stupidity or even want of personal courage," and asserts that "eternal defeat and miscarriage must attend the man of the best parts if cursed with indecision." This is all. Reed however says: "*It is entirely owing to you that this army, and the liberties of America so far as they are dependent on it, are not totally cut off. You have decision, a quality often wanted in minds otherwise valuable.*" "*I have no doubt, had you been here, the garrison of Fort Washington would now have composed part of this army.*"

He adds that Washington's mind remained in a state of suspense till the blow was struck, and philosophizes: "Oh! General, *an indecisive mind is one of the greatest misfortunes that can befall an army; how often have I lamented it in this campaign!*"

The following extract from Washington's reply of the 14th June, shows that his confidence was completely restored by reason of the deceit which was thus practised upon him :—

"I thank you most sincerely for the friendly and affectionate sentiments contained in yours of the 4th inst., and assure you that I am perfectly convinced of the sincerity of them. True it is, *I felt myself hurt by a certain letter which appeared at that time to be the* ECHO *of one from you.* I was hurt, not because I thought my judgment wronged by the expressions contained in it, but because the same sentiments were not communicated immediately to myself. The favorable manner in which your opinions upon all occasions had been received, the impression they made, and the unreserved manner in which I wished, and required them to be given, entitled me, I thought, to your advice upon any point in which I appeared to be wanting. To meet with anything, then, that carried with it a complexion of *withholding that advice from me, and censuring my conduct to another, was such an argument of disingenuity, that I was not a little mortified at it. However, I am perfectly satisfied that matters were not as they appeared from the letter alluded to.*"

"From this moment," says Mr. Wm. B. Reed, "such was the influence of FRANK and MANLY explanations, all distrust and apparent estrangement were removed, and the ancient relations of friendly confidence effectually restored."

A fear that Lee would publish his letter must have been the bane of Reed's existence, and he appears to have taken considerable pains, by friendly assurances, to prevent it; for, on the 22d July, 1778, after the battle of Monmouth, in reply to what must have been an effort of this kind, Lee says to him :—

"I am pleased in your having confirmed me in the opinion I had entertained of your regard and friendship, and I am sorry that you should suppose me for a single moment capable of availing myself of some expressions you had made use of in a confidential letter, to embroil you with a man that the public interest certainly and perhaps your personal concerns, render it necessary you should be on good terms with."

General Reed, however, prudently saved himself from the discredit of being a personal friend of such an unpopular man, by informing General Greene, in a "*confidential*" letter dated 5th Nov. 1778, that as to General Lee and himself "We are utterly out. After laboring to convince me he had great merit at Monmouth, and I to convince him that he had behaved very ill, which I knew from his own mouth and my own observations"—observations which must have antedated the letter that had so pleased Lee—"we have parted mutually unconvinced. I only added one piece of advice to him, to forbear any reflections on the Commander-in-chief."

Nothing but the strongest confidence in his ability

to maintain Lee's secrecy, or a belief that the letter
had been lost, could have emboldened General Reed,
in the summer of 1779, to make in print, and forward
to Washington, the following unblushing assertions :—

"In the fall of 1776, I was extremely anxious that Fort Washington should be evacuated; there was a difference in opinion
among those whom the General consulted, and he hesitated more
than I ever knew him on any other occasion, and more than I
thought the public service admitted. Knowing that General Lee's
opinion would be a great support to mine, I wrote to him from
Hackensack, stating the case, and my reasons, and, I think, urg-
ing him to join me in sentiment at the close of my letter; and,
alluding to the particular subject then before me, to the best of
my recollection, I added this sentence: 'With a thousand good
and great qualities, there is a want of decision to complete the
perfect military character.' Upon this sentence, or one to this
effect, wrote in haste, in full confidence, and in great anxiety for
the event, is this ungenerous sentiment introduced into the world.
The event but too fully justified my anxiety; for the fort was summoned that very day, and surrendered the next. I absolutely
deny that there is any other ground but this letter; and if there
is, let it be produced. I have now only to add that, though General Washington soon after, by an accident, knew of this circumstance, it never lessened the friendship which subsisted between
us. He had too much greatness of mind to suppose himself inca-
pable of mistake, or to dislike a faithful friend who should note
an error with such circumstances of respect, and on such an
occasion."

All the assertions of this letter are so amazing
that it is impossible to mark the worst ones by italics.
The possession of a "thousand great and good quali-

ties" and an "otherwise perfect military character"
had never been ascribed to Washington by Reed, and
as Fort Washington had surrendered five days before
the letter was written, its design could hardly have
been to secure a confirmatory opinion from Lee as to
the propriety of an evacuation.

Washington's friendship has ever been as a tower
of strength to General Reed; but, obtained by false
pretences like those unveiled, it reflects but little
lustre upon the latter. The trustfulness of Washington's nature rendered him peculiarly susceptible to
the arts of those who surrounded him. General Reed
himself, in one of his letters, thus cautions him
against this weakness of which he afterwards so suc-
cessfully availed himself: "Do not let the goodness
of your heart subject you to the influence of opinions
from men in every respect your inferiors." There is
reason to believe, from the entire cessation of correspondence and otherwise, that in the year 1781
Washington became acquainted with the deception
which had been practised upon him. On the 16th
day of June, 1781, Lee wrote a letter to Mr. Morris
"filled," according to Mr. Wm. B. Reed, "with viru-
lent denunciations of Mr. Reed and his friends."
The thunder of his denunciations was most probably
accompanied by the lightning's flash that revealed to
Washington the "Scarlet Letter." To General
Greene, on the 1st Nov. 1781, General Reed com-
plains that "the incessant misrepresentations and

calumnies with respect to myself, and some un-
friendly characters about him, have raised some pre-
judices, of what nature I cannot tell."*

Washington's much relied upon letter to Reed, of
the 15th September, 1782, written in compliance with
the latter's pressing request, by its freezing tone, its
non-responsiveness, its reference to a *past* confidence
alone, its lack of indignation at the charges against
the latter, and an absence of those closing words of
affection which marked its writer's earlier correspondence, makes the conjecture of this discovery almost a
certainty. Its probability is not affected by the fact
that in an *official* escort furnished Washington when
he left Philadelphia in March, 1782, Gen. Reed,
whose Presidency had expired only two months previously, was included. Mr. Reed must have felt hard
driven when he hunted for this straw, through the
dusty files of the "Freeman's Journal."†

SIXTH. As to the opinion of Dr. Rush, entertained
by his cotemporaries.

Under the plea of "utter unfitness" for the task, to
which none will demur who have witnessed the result
of his labors upon some of them, Mr. Reed ignores

* Forgetful of this evidence, Mr. Reed says, " With this exception (a
letter from his grandfather to Mrs. Reed alluding to Washington's cold-
ness) *I do not find the least trace of the difference* which the busy and
malevolent men of the day have insinuated."

† Reed's Reply, page 122.

the principal portions of Dr. Rush's life, and undertakes an investigation, similar in kind, however dissimilar in results, to that of Professor Owen in determining the structure of the Mastodon from one of its teeth. As eminence in the medical profession, whose practitioners are brought into daily contact with the pains and sorrows of life and the stern realities of death, has been seldom found conjoined with the disposition attributed to Dr. Rush, it was impossible to arrive at a correct estimate of his moral character, without considering his merits and career as a physician. Belittling observations with his reversed telescope should therefore have contented Mr. Reed, without any previous quartering of the object to be viewed.

Truly, and not *sneeringly*, may it be said of Dr. Rush, in view of the incessant study by which he stored his mind with its immense fund of knowledge; of the labor and toil with which he assisted in laying the foundations for the world-wide fame of the Philadelphia medical schools; of his contributions to science; of his writings, translated into many tongues, rewarded by the crowned heads of Europe with medals and by the leading scientific men of his time with the warmest encomiums; of his active participation in the humane institutions of this city; of his bold and successful confronting of an epidemic in whose terrible presence men stood spell-bound, or before whose ravages they fled in terror; of his large and wearying practice—that he was a "*busy*" man.

Even in his brief political career, to which Mr. Reed has so slightingly referred, and which was only an episode in his "busy" life, he distinguished himself greatly, as a man of strong, decided character, an unflinching patriot, an ardent worshipper of liberty.

In the "Edinburgh Encyclopædia" it is stated: "In June, 1776, he was a member of the Provincial Conference which met at Philadelphia, and, on the 23d day of that month, moved for a committee to draft an address expressive of the sense of the Conference respecting the independence of the American Colonies. Dr. Rush, who, with James Smith and Thomas McKean, had been appointed for this purpose, the next day reported a Declaration, which was adopted in the Conference and presented to the American Congress the day after. This Declaration, even its phraseology, anticipated almost the whole of the Declaration of Independence."

Dr. Rush, with others, was elected to Congress for the express purpose of signing the Declaration of Independence. He there laid or broadened the foundations of life-long friendships with many of the immortal men of American history, amongst others with Thomas Jefferson and John Adams, between whom, shortly before his death, he effected a reconciliation, and with whom, through long years of bitter political dissensions, he ever preserved the most intimate relations.

His foresight and statesmanlike breadth of view, may be gathered from a speech he delivered in Congress, in July, 1776, in the course of which he said:—

"We represent the people; we are a *nation;* to vote by States will keep up colonial distinctions; and we shall be loath to admit new colonies into the confederation. The voting by the number of free inhabitants will have the excellent effect of inducing the Colonies to discourage slavery. If we vote by numbers, liberty will always be safe; the larger Colonies are so providentially divided in situation as to render any fear of their combining visionary. *The more a man aims at serving America, the more he serves his colony; I am not pleading the cause of Pennsylvania; I consider myself a citizen of America.*"

The spontaneous tributes of respect which were cast upon Dr. Rush's grave whilst the memory of his virtues and the grief for his loss were still fresh, were paid to those features of character most inconsistent with the existence of defects such as those alleged by Mr. Reed. These features too were selected because they were salient ones, and not because they had been impeached or assailed; for, until the advent of Mr. Reed, no one had been found, so reckless of that charity to the dead he had himself so frequently invoked, of the feelings of the living with whom he was on terms of social intimacy, of the statements, aye, more, of the *truth* of history, as to assert of Dr. Rush that he was "utterly unworthy of belief."

In " Rees' Cyclopædia" is found this passage :—

" Above his eminence, said the Rev. Dr. Staughton, as a patriot and physician, rose his character as a Christian. Convinced of the truth of the Scriptures, he endeavored to promote their universal circulation. His defence of the Bible as a school-book, written at a time when infidelity carried a more brazen front than at the present day, has been highly beneficial to his country. He was a prime mover of the Phila-delphia Bible Society, the first established in the United States. He was uniform in the discharge of Christian duties, and died professing a hope in the Saviour of sinners."

In the " Encyclopædia Americana" it is said : " He was moreover philanthropic, kind, and religious."

In the "New American Cyclopædia" that: "He had the highest reverence for the Holy Scriptures, and was equally distinguished for his piety as for his learning."

The celebrated Dr. Hosack, in an address before the College of Physicians and Surgeons, delivered on the 3d Nov. 1813, said :—

" But the virtues of the heart, like the faculties of his mind, were also in continued exercise for the benefit of his fellow men, while the numerous humane, charitable, and religious associations which do honor to the city of Philadelphia, bear testimony to the philanthropy and piety which animated the bosom of their departed benefactor; let it also be remembered that, as with the Good Samaritan, the poor were the objects of his peculiar care, and that in the latter and more prosperous years of his life, one-seventh of his income was expended upon the children of affliction and want. The last act of Dr. Rush was an act of charity, and the last expression which fell from his lips was an injunction to his son, 'Be indulgent to the poor.'"

Dr. David Ramsay, in an address before the Medical Society of South Carolina at Charleston, in June, 1813, said:—

"Piety to God was an eminent trait in the character of Dr. Rush. In all his printed works and in all his private transactions he expressed the most profound respect and veneration for the great Eternal."

In Thacher's "American Medical Biography" it is stated that "Dr. Rush readily forgave injuries and the ingratitude of those on whom he had conferred favors."

Dr. Francis, in the course of an Address before the Rutgers' Medical Faculty, which has been incorporated into many of the standard biographies and encyclopædias, said:—

"There are other qualities which entitle Dr. Rush to our respect and esteem. In private life his disposition and deportment were in the highest degree exemplary. Admired and courted for his intellectual endowments, he riveted the affections of all those who enjoyed the pleasure of an intimate acquaintance. The affability of his manners, the amiableness of his temper, and the benevolence of his character, were ever conspicuous. He was ardent in his friendships, and forgiving in his resentments; and yet entertaining a due regard for himself and a nice sense of honor, he possessed a manly independence of spirit, which disdained everything mean and servile. He had an extraordinary command of language, and always imparted his thoughts in a peculiarly impressive and eloquent manner. His eloquence as a public teacher surpassed that of all his contemporaries.

"He never evinced any of that haughtiness and affectation of importance which sometimes attach to men of eminence. He was a believer in Christianity from an examination of its principles and the deepest conviction. The purity of its doctrines and the excellence of its precepts were a frequent topic of his conversation; its practical influence upon his conduct through life he often acknowledged, and cherished with a fervent hope the animating prospects it affords. With the good old Bishop Burnet he fully coincided, 'that a man living according to the rules of religion, becomes the wisest, the best, the happiest creature he is capable of being.' His writings in numerous places bear testimony to his Christian virtues; he designed to conclude his literary and professional labors with a distinct work on the medicine of the Bible; and in a letter written a short time before his fatal illness he candidly declares that he had acquired and received nothing from the world which he so highly prized, as the religious principles he received from his parents. To inculcate those principles which flow from the source of all truth and purity, and to impart them as a legacy to his children, was an object dear to his heart, and which he never failed to promote by constant exhortation, and the powerful influence of his own example."

Jefferson, in a letter to John Adams of the 27th May, 1813, announcing Dr. Rush's death, says:—

"Another of our patriots of '76 is gone, my dear sir, another of the Signers of the Independence of our country. And a better man than Rush could not have left us, more benevolent, more learned, of finer genius, or more honest."

It is not deemed necessary to quote further from the immense mass of similar testimony at hand, inasmuch as no eulogium of Dr. Rush is here designed.

In conclusion, it is greatly to be hoped, that when next Mr. Reed assumes the *offensive defensive*, his production will be a little the latter and not so exclusively the former, and further, that his great powers will be exercised in behalf of a more worthy person than the one who admitted of himself in one of those spasms of truth with which the most mendacious are sometimes seized, that he was "*not worth purchasing,*" and whose want of importance was such that Mr. Bancroft, when summoned by his advocate (Reed's Reply, p. 84), was compelled to say :—

"In looking through the archives here (London) which have been opened to me with great liberality, *I have looked for traces of your grandfather, but as yet have found nothing of much importance.*"

And the ever friendly Mr. Sparks, who would have found it difficult to count the number of times the name of Washington was mentioned, to testify:—

"In the public offices in London I have examined all the correspondence between the British officers in America and the Ministers during the war. I have no recollection of seeing *General Reed's name mentioned in these papers on any occasion.*"

www.ingramcontent.com/pod-product-compliance
Lightning Source LLC
Chambersburg PA
CBHW021630270326
41931CB00008B/961